Surviving the
HURRICANE

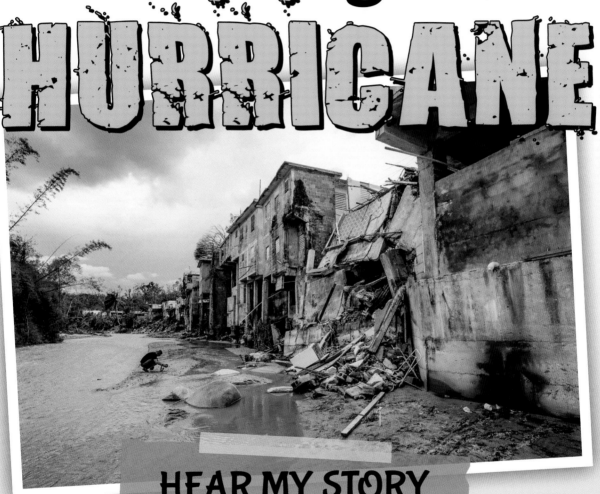

HEAR MY STORY

Heather C. Hudak

CRABTREE
PUBLISHING COMPANY
WWW.CRABTREEBOOKS.COM

Author: Heather C. Hudak

Editorial director: Kathy Middleton

Editors: Sarah Eason, Jennifer Sanderson, and Ellen Rodger

Proofreaders: Tracey Kelly, Melissa Boyce

Editorial director: Kathy Middleton

Design: Paul Myerscough

Cover design: Margaret Amy Salter

Photo research: Rachel Blount

Production coordinator and Prepress technician: Tammy McGarr

Print coordinator: Katherine Berti

Consultant: John Farndon

Produced for Crabtree Publishing Company by Calcium

Photo Credits:
t=Top, c=Center, b=Bottom, l= Left, r=Right

Inside: Shutterstock: AMFPhotography: p. 20; Pamela Brick: pp. 28-29; Cindy Camperlengo: p. 8; CaseSensitiveFilms: p. 29r; Chris Rivera86: pp. 1, 16-17; Dejan-Milosavljevic: p. 9; FotoKina: p. 10; Malachi Jacobs: pp. 6-7; Joseph: p. 13r; Terry Kelly: p. 5; Nejron Photo: p. 14; Trong Nguyen: p. 4; NorthStarPhotos: p. 27; Alessandro Pietri: p. 18; Joseph Sohm: p. 26; Stockphotofan1: pp. 12-13; Robert Szymanski: p. 19; Udaix: p. 11t; Vicbruno: p. 7r; Ymphotos: p. 15; Wikimedia Commons: Air Force Magazine: p. 17b; FEMA/Mark Wolfe: p. 11b; Anthony Ivanoff: p. 21; NASA - Terra MODIS Satellite: p. 25; NOAA/NASA: p. 24; Roosevelt Skerrit from Vieille Case, Dominica: pp. 22-23, 23t.

Cover: Shutterstock

Publisher's Note: The story presented in this book is a fictional account based on extensive research of real-life accounts, with the aim of reflecting the true experience of victims of natural disasters.

Library and Archives Canada Cataloguing in Publication

Title: Surviving the hurricane : hear my story / Heather C. Hudak.
Names: Hudak, Heather C., 1975- author.
Description: Series statement: Disaster diaries | Includes index.
Identifiers: Canadiana (print) 20200150154 |
  Canadiana (ebook) 20200150162 |
  ISBN 9780778769903 (hardcover) |
  ISBN 9780778771180 (softcover) |
  ISBN 9781427124470 (HTML)
Subjects: LCSH: Hurricane Maria, 2017—Juvenile literature. |
  LCSH: Hurricanes—Puerto Rico—Juvenile literature. |
  LCSH: Hurricanes—Juvenile literature. |
  LCSH: Disaster victims—Juvenile literature.
Classification: LCC QC994.2 .H83 2020 | DDC j55155/2097295—dc23

Library of Congress Cataloging-in-Publication Data

Names: Hudak, Heather C., 1975- author.
Title: Surviving the hurricane : hear my story / Heather C. Hudak.
Description: New York : Crabtree Publishing Company, [2020] |
  Series: Disaster diaries |
  Includes bibliographical references and index.
Identifiers: LCCN 2019053355 (print) | LCCN 2019053356 (ebook) |
  ISBN 9780778769903 (hardcover) |
  ISBN 9780778771180 (paperback) |
  ISBN 9781427124470 (ebook)
Subjects: LCSH: Hurricane Maria, 2017--Juvenile literature. |
  Disaster victims--Puerto Rico--Juvenile literature. |
  Disaster relief--Puerto Rico--Juvenile literature.
Classification: LCC HV636 2017 .P9 H83 2020 (print) |
  LCC HV636 2017 .P9 (ebook) | DDC 363.34/922092 [B]--dc23
LC record available at https://lccn.loc.gov/2019053355
LC ebook record available at https://lccn.loc.gov/2019053356

Crabtree Publishing Company

www.crabtreebooks.com   1-800-387-7650

Printed in the U.S.A./022020/CG20200102

Published in Canada
Crabtree Publishing
616 Welland Ave.
St. Catharines, Ontario
L2M 5V6

Published in the United States
Crabtree Publishing
PMB 59051
350 Fifth Avenue, 59th Floor
New York, New York 10118

Published in the United Kingdom
Crabtree Publishing
Maritime House
Basin Road North, Hove
BN41 1WR

Published in Australia
Crabtree Publishing
3 Charles Street
Coburg North
VIC, 3058

Contents

Hurricanes and Their Victims

Hurricanes are massive, spiral-shaped **tropical storms** that spin around and around. They form over oceans, and when they hit land they can cause terrible damage. Weather forecasting helps people know if a hurricane is heading their way. But some people may remain in the area anyway. Some cannot afford to leave, or there may be no safe way to **evacuate**. Others may choose not to leave their homes.

Dangerous Winds

Hurricane winds gust at speeds greater than 74 miles per hour (119 kph). At sea, hurricane winds cause water levels to rise and huge waves to form. When these waves hit the shoreline, they cause flooding and other damage in coastal **communities**.

Satellites in space capture images of hurricanes, such as this one of Hurricane Irma on September 8, 2017.

Dangers on Land

When hurricanes make landfall, or reach land, their winds blast everything in their path. They tear through buildings, leaving them in piles of rubble. Hurricanes also damage the natural environment. They rip trees and other plants from the ground, tossing them around in the air. The thunderstorms that hurricanes bring cause heavy rainfall that can lead to flooding. Often, the flooding causes more damage than the wind.

People in Mexico Beach, Florida, were left homeless, without food, money, medication, and identification when Hurricane Michael struck in 2018.

Name Changer

"Hurricane" is the word used to describe extreme tropical storms that form in the North Atlantic Ocean and the eastern North Pacific Ocean. However, they are known by different names depending on where they develop. They are known as typhoons if they form in the western North Pacific Ocean near China, Japan, and the Philippines. They are called cyclones if they form in the South Pacific and the Indian Ocean.

ANTONIO'S STORY

In this book, you can find out what it is like to live through a **natural disaster** by reading the **fictional** story of Antonio, a young boy caught up in the Hurricane Maria disaster in Puerto Rico. Look for his story on pages 6–7, 12–13, 16–17, 22–23, and 28–29.

ANTONIO'S STORY:
A Hurricane Is Coming

My name is Antonio Vega. I am 13 years old, and I live in a small fishing village called Naguabo, in Puerto Rico. My village is hundreds of years old. It stretches from the Caribbean Sea to the Luquillo Mountain Range. Naguabo is one of the main entry points to the El Yunque rain forest. I often take my little brother into the forest at night to look for coqui frogs and glowing insects. We gaze at the stars and listen to the sounds of the animals all around us.

People come from far and wide to swim at our beautiful beaches. My friend's father used to own a small tour company. He would take people snorkeling off the coast. He always served a meal of fresh seafood caught by local fishers. My father is one of these fishers. At least, he was, before Hurricane Maria destroyed much of Naguabo in September 2017.

Naguabo is nicknamed el Pueblo de los Enchumbaos, or "The Town of the Drenched," for the large amounts of rain the town gets each year.

Maria was the worst hurricane to hit Puerto Rico in more than 80 years. My village was one of the first places in Puerto Rico that the storm hit. It was also one of the worst damaged.

Years have passed since that terrible time, but I remember it like it was yesterday. Storms had been brewing for weeks, and news about hurricanes in the area was a part of our daily lives. Just a few weeks earlier, Hurricane Irma passed north of Puerto Rico. It did not hit our island, but it still caused hundreds of millions of dollars in damage and killed four people. Tens of thousands of people were without power. We hoped that was the worst we would see on our island—but we were wrong.

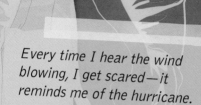

Every time I hear the wind blowing, I get scared—it reminds me of the hurricane.

The loud song of male coqui frogs fills the forests. It sounds like they are saying, "co-kee!"

DANGER

Trails of Destruction

Heavy rain and high waves wash away bridges and roads and flood entire communities.

The rain, winds, and flooding that hurricanes bring have a disastrous effect on the natural environment, people, animals, and human-made structures. Each year, approximately 10,000 people die in hurricanes and tropical storms around the world.

Water World

Flooding is the largest cause of death during a hurricane. Huge downpours of rain can bring inches of water to an area in just a day or two. Local bodies of water begin to overflow. **Levees** may break too. Hurricanes also cause seawater levels to rise. This gradual rise in sea level is known as a **storm surge**. Storm surges can flood coastal communities, causing horrific damage and destruction.

Property Damage

Hurricanes cause extensive damage to property. Depending on the size of the storm, roofs can be torn from buildings and houses can be flattened. Overhead power lines and communications systems are often knocked out, leaving people without electricity or the means to contact one another.

Environmental Impact

During a hurricane, sand is swept from coastal areas and **deposited** elsewhere. This is an issue for birds, turtles, and other animals that nest in the sand. Massive waves bring salty ocean water ashore, which mixes with **freshwater** rivers and streams. Floodwaters also cause mudslides and can move large rocks. All of these activities force changes in the local **ecosystem**.

Animal Victims

Hurricanes also impact wildlife. Corals may break as a result of the winds, and fish need to work harder to swim against rough waters. Some birds sense storms and fly away. Marine animals often swim to deeper water. Land animals such as snakes may burrow into the ground, while deer run in search of safety. However, animals such as cattle may not be able to escape the storm.

VICTIMS OF THE DEBRIS

Flying or falling **debris** is a real danger during and after hurricanes. In Cuba in 2017, three people were killed by falling debris as a result of Hurricane Irma. Two victims were killed when a balcony fell on top of the bus they were in. The third was killed by a fallen electrical pole.

People should always take their pets with them during a hurricane evacuation. Situations that are not safe for people are not safe for pets either.

How Hurricanes Work

Hurricanes have three main parts: the eye, the eye wall, and rainbands. The eye is the center of the hurricane and the calmest part. The eye wall surrounds the eye and is the most destructive part. Rainbands are clouds that spiral from the eye wall to make the storm larger in size.

Size and Speed

In a small hurricane, winds extend about 25 miles (40 km) from the eye of the storm. This number jumps to about 150 miles (241 km) for a large hurricane. However, the size of a hurricane does not determine how much damage it can cause. The damage depends on the wind speed and where the hurricane makes landfall. For example, the damage will be worse if the hurricane makes landfall over a city.

Hurricane Categories

Meteorologists are scientists who study the weather. They use the Saffir–Simpson Hurricane Wind Scale (SSHWS) to measure a hurricane's strength. There are five categories of hurricane on the SSHWS, and each one brings a different level of destruction. The chart on page 11 shows the different categories and the level of destruction each category causes.

Hurricane Irma lasted from August 31 to September 11, 2017. It caused about $50 billion in damages.

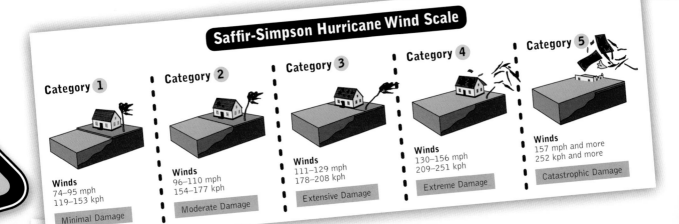

Saffir-Simpson Hurricane Wind Scale

Category 1
Winds
74–95 mph
119–153 kph
Minimal Damage

Category 2
Winds
96–110 mph
154–177 kph
Moderate Damage

Category 3
Winds
111–129 mph
178–208 kph
Extensive Damage

Category 4
Winds
130–156 mph
209–251 kph
Extreme Damage

Category 5
Winds
157 mph and more
252 kph and more
Catastrophic Damage

What's in a Name?

Until the 1950s, hurricanes were tracked by the year in which they took place. However, it was difficult to keep track of storms that took place at the same time. Now they are given unique names based on a list created by the World Meteorological Association. The list of appropriate names can be reused every six years. If a storm is especially noteworthy, its name is removed from the list and not reused. For example, "Katrina" and "Maria" will never be used again.

VICTIMS OF THE FLOOD

In August 2005, Hurricane Katrina struck the southeastern United States. Katrina was a Category 5 hurricane and was the costliest and one of the deadliest hurricanes in U.S. history. It caused more than $160 million in damages and killed more than 1,800 people. The levees around New Orleans, Louisiana, failed to hold back the storm surge, so it broke through, causing horrific floods to the area.

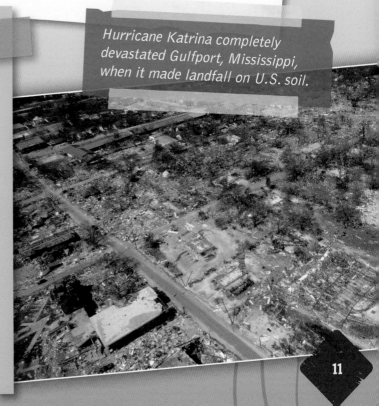

Hurricane Katrina completely devastated Gulfport, Mississippi, when it made landfall on U.S. soil.

11

ANTONIO'S STORY:
Fleeing to Safety

We watched the news each day to see if any more storms were headed our way. Two days before Maria struck land, the governor of Puerto Rico sent out an evacuation order. He warned people in flood-prone parts of the country to find a safe place to ride out the storm. I knew this is what hurricanes were like from stories told by my family, but it was still hard to believe.

The government opened 450 shelters to house 125,000 people across Puerto Rico. My parents knew we needed to get to one of them to ensure our safety. They told us to pack a small bag with a few items. They spent the next day or so boarding up the doors and windows of our house and securing my father's fishing boat.

Then we got in our car and drove north toward an inland shelter. It was clear that others had the same idea. There was a long line of cars waiting to fill up at the gas station. It took nearly an hour for us to reach the front of the line, and when we did, there was only enough fuel left to fill half the tank. We hoped it would be enough.

Maria tore off roofs, stripped trees bare, and flooded many areas.

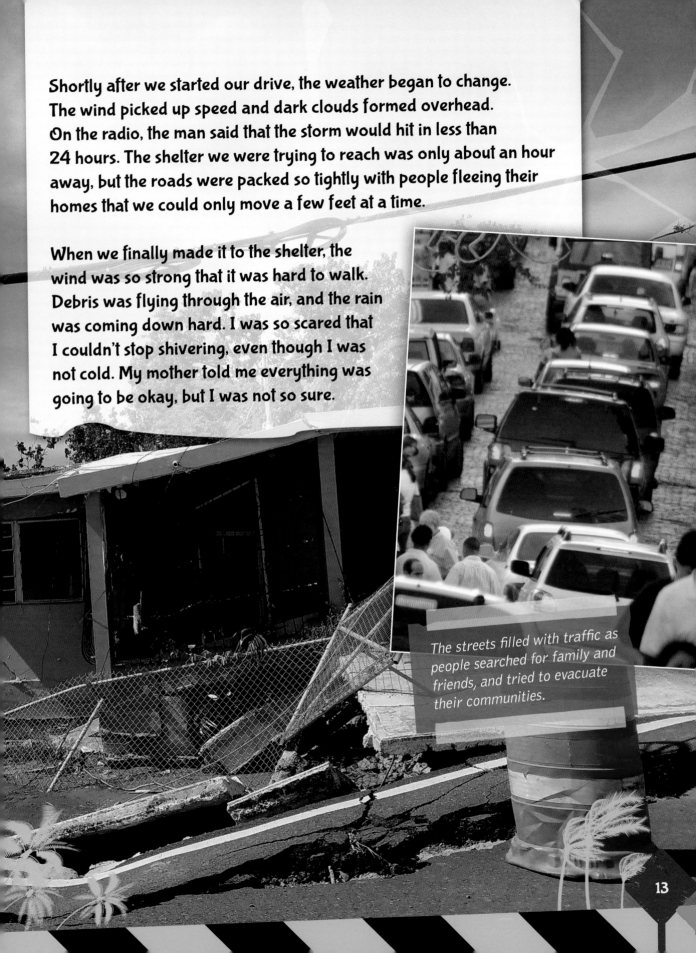

Shortly after we started our drive, the weather began to change. The wind picked up speed and dark clouds formed overhead. On the radio, the man said that the storm would hit in less than 24 hours. The shelter we were trying to reach was only about an hour away, but the roads were packed so tightly with people fleeing their homes that we could only move a few feet at a time.

When we finally made it to the shelter, the wind was so strong that it was hard to walk. Debris was flying through the air, and the rain was coming down hard. I was so scared that I couldn't stop shivering, even though I was not cold. My mother told me everything was going to be okay, but I was not so sure.

The streets filled with traffic as people searched for family and friends, and tried to evacuate their communities.

The Causes of Hurricanes

Hurricanes start out as a cluster of clouds called tropical disturbances. Not all tropical disturbances become hurricanes. The conditions need to be just right. Just like making a cake, you need to have all the right ingredients. The main ingredients are warm water and moist, warm air. Once a hurricane forms, it needs a constant supply of these ingredients to maintain itself. As long as they are available, the hurricane will grow.

Water Energy

Water acts like fuel for a tropical storm. It supplies the energy the storm needs to grow and become a hurricane. The temperature of the water needs to be at least 79 °Fahrenheit (26 °C) for a tropical storm to turn into a hurricane.

About 12 hours before a hurricane hits an area, thick clouds form in the sky and there is heavy rainfall.

VICTIMS OF THE STORM SURGE

In November 2013, Typhoon Haiyan had a terrible impact on the Philippines. The typhoon created a storm surge that killed more than 6,000 people. It was the deadliest typhoon that the country had ever seen.

Rising Air

As warm, moist air rises from the surface of the water, it creates an area of lower **pressure** beneath it. Air from other areas blows to take the place of the rising air. The new air begins to rise too, and more air blows in. The rising air cools over time, forming clouds from the water in the air. This cycle continues over and over again without any pauses or breaks.

Growing Storm

As time goes on, more and more clouds form, fed by the warm water and moist air below. If there is enough warm water, wind, and moist air, the wind speeds will increase, and storm clouds grow to form a hurricane. It can take from hours to days for a tropical disturbance to become a hurricane. However, hurricanes cannot sustain themselves without their main ingredients. This means that they begin to die as they hit land or cooler waters.

Typhoon Haiyan killed thousands of people and left 4 million people homeless.

ANTONIO'S STORY:

Riding out the Storm

The shelter we stayed in was a sports arena made of **reinforced** steel and concrete. We were each given a cot on the lowest level and told to stay put. My mother had packed a deck of cards and told my brother and me to play a game. She wanted to help keep our minds off the storm, but it was all I could think about.

The man on the cot next to mine was listening to a radio. The woman on the radio said the storm had grown to a Category 5 hurricane and would destroy everything it touched. As the storm got closer, we were told to stay away from the windows and doors. The lights began to flicker. The wind and rain were howling loudly. We knew when the worst was near because the entire building began to shake.

We held each other close and prayed we would make it out alive. Parts of the ceiling crumbled and rain leaked in around us. The glass from the windows shattered, and the doors were ripped off the building. We could hear what sounded like fireworks going off, but it was the overhead power lines falling down. The storm lasted for hours, but we were all together, and that was all that mattered.

In some parts of Puerto Rico, floodwaters were more than 30 inches (76 cm) deep and filled with sewage.

We waited for a while after the storm passed before we moved. We sat there holding each other. We were so thankful to be alive and too scared to look outside at what we knew must be total destruction.

Some people had been hurt when larger debris and some of the falling ceiling hit them, but they would be okay. They mainly had small cuts and bruises that would heal quickly. My mother held my brother and me at arm's length and checked us over from head to toe to make sure we were not hurt anywhere. Then she kissed our heads at least a dozen times. She had tears streaming down her face.

Maria knocked out power sources across Puerto Rico. People had limited access to clean water and food after the hurricane.

Where Hurricanes Happen

Hurricanes start over **tropical** waters near the equator. About 90 percent of tropical storms form within 20 degrees **latitude** of the equator. Beyond that, the surface temperature of the water is too cool. The Peru Current and the Benguela Current are the only two places within typical hurricane zones where the water is too cool year round for hurricanes to form.

Hurricane Basins

Hurricanes are more common in some parts of the world than others. The seven key areas where hurricanes tend to form are called hurricane **basins**. They are the Atlantic, Eastern Pacific/Central Pacific, Northwest Pacific, North Indian, Southwest Indian, Australian/Southeast Indian, and Australian/Southwest Pacific.

Hurricane Maria was the tenth-strongest Atlantic hurricane in recorded history.

Countries in Danger

There are more hurricanes in the Pacific Ocean than any other place on Earth. The most powerful storms take place in the Western Pacific. The Indian Ocean comes in second and the Atlantic Ocean, third.

Some countries are more likely than others to be hit by a tropical storm or hurricane due to their location. The 10 countries most likely to experience a hurricane are China, the Philippines, Japan, Mexico, the United States, Australia, Taiwan, Vietnam, Madagascar, and Cuba. Within the United States, the Atlantic Coast, the Gulf of Mexico, and the Hawaiian Islands are at the biggest risk of hurricanes.

In 2016, Hurricane Matthew tore through Freeport in the Bahamas, causing mass destruction. Winds reached speeds of 121 miles per hour (195 kph).

VICTIMS OF REPETITION

Abaco in the Bahamas has been affected by hurricanes 82 times since 1871. This is more than any other place in the coastal United States, Mexico, and the Caribbean Islands. In September 2004, Abaco was hit by two hurricanes, Frances and Jeanne, within 22 days of each other. On September 1, 2019, Abaco was hit by Hurricane Dorian. The Category 5 storm was the worst to ever touch land on Abaco. Much of the island was devastated. Dozens of people were killed and thousands were left homeless. After Dorian, thousands of people left the island by boat or plane.

Dangerous Times

Typically, hurricanes take place during the warm season. However, they can occur any time the conditions are right. Still, they are more likely to appear at certain times of year. The hurricane season varies from one part of the world to another. Before the start of the hurricane season, meteorologists begin to make predictions. They make guesses about the types of storms that may take place, how many there will be, and where they will hit.

Rockport, Texas, took a direct hit from Hurricane Harvey in August 2017. The town lost about 20 percent of its population as a result of the storm.

Storm Season

In general, the Northern Hemisphere hurricane season runs from April through December, depending on the location. In the Southern Hemisphere, it runs from November through April. However, each of the seven hurricane basins has its own hurricane season. In every basin, hurricane season reaches its peak in the late summer months. Typically, more hurricanes take place in September than any other month, while May has the fewest hurricanes.

Northwest Pacific Basin

Hurricane season takes place year round in the Northwest Pacific. It accounts for about 30 percent of all hurricanes that take place on Earth.

Eastern Pacific Basin

In the Eastern Pacific basin, hurricane season starts on May 15 and runs until November 30. The worst storms in these basins usually take place from July to September. In an average year, the Eastern Pacific basin is the second most active hurricane basin.

North Indian Basin

In the North Indian basin, hurricanes can happen year round. They typically take place from April to December. There are two peaks in the season, one in May and the other in November.

The North Indian basin usually has fewer hurricanes per year than the other basins. However, they are some of the most deadly. Hurricanes in this region often kill thousands of people because they tend to strike land in densely populated parts of Bangladesh, Pakistan, and India.

VICTIMS OF CHANGE

The year 2018 was one of the most active hurricane seasons on record. **Climate change** is one reason for the increase in hurricanes. In the Northern Hemisphere, 22 major hurricanes struck land in just 70 days. In the North Atlantic, Hurricane Florence was only a Category 1 when it hit land. However, it brought heavy rainfalls, resulting in 48 deaths, $60 billion in damages, and the loss of power for millions of people. In the Western Pacific, Category 5 Typhoon Mangkhut killed 60 people when it hit land.

When Typhoon Mangkhut hit land in Hong Kong, more than 1,500 trees were uprooted.

ANTONIO'S STORY:
Total Loss

We wanted to see the damage for ourselves. My mother took my hand and my father held my brother's hand as we all walked together to the nearest door. What we saw was worse than anything we could have imagined. The landscape was empty as far as our eyes could see. All the trees and grass had been uprooted. Most buildings were flattened to the ground. Those that were still standing were crumbling and unstable. The roofs were ripped off of houses and the houses were flooded.

I immediately began to wonder what our house looked like. We lived so much closer to the water, where the hurricane first hit. I was sure there would be nothing left. I tried to hold back my tears, but I could not stop thinking about our friends and family, and if they had made it to safety. I began to sob.

Hurricane Maria caused about $94 billion in damages across Puerto Rico.

DANGER

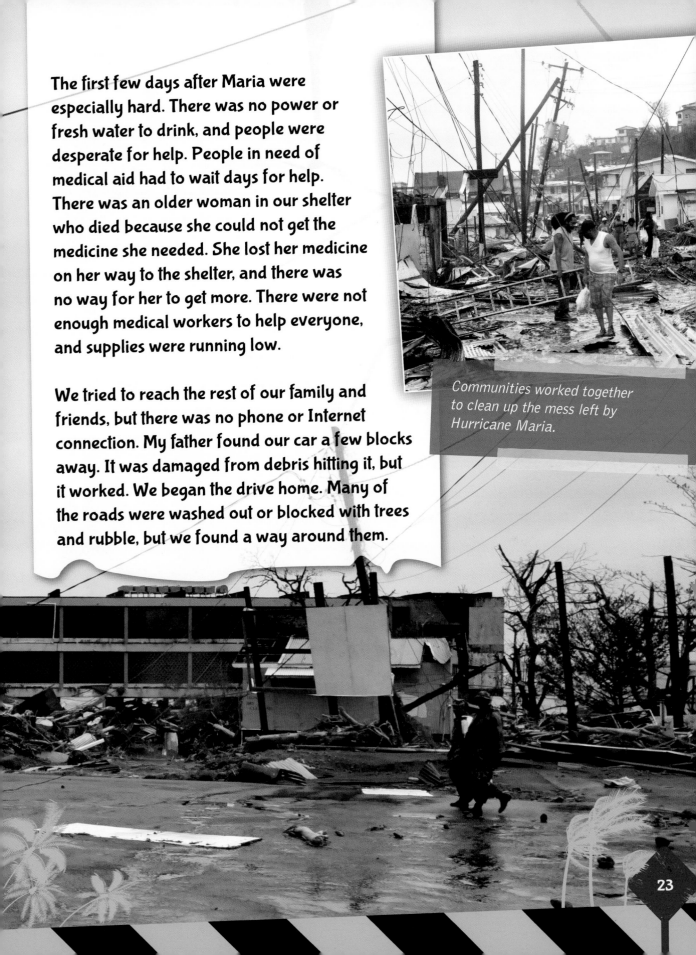

The first few days after Maria were especially hard. There was no power or fresh water to drink, and people were desperate for help. People in need of medical aid had to wait days for help. There was an older woman in our shelter who died because she could not get the medicine she needed. She lost her medicine on her way to the shelter, and there was no way for her to get more. There were not enough medical workers to help everyone, and supplies were running low.

We tried to reach the rest of our family and friends, but there was no phone or Internet connection. My father found our car a few blocks away. It was damaged from debris hitting it, but it worked. We began the drive home. Many of the roads were washed out or blocked with trees and rubble, but we found a way around them.

Communities worked together to clean up the mess left by Hurricane Maria.

23

How Science Can Fight Hurricanes

Scientists are always looking for ways to provide people with advance warning of **potential** hurricanes. The earlier people know that a major hurricane is headed their way, the better they can prepare for it.

Carbon Dating

Scientists use technology, such as **carbon-14 dating**, to study soil samples in areas that have been hit by hurricanes. During a hurricane, storm surges push sand onto the shore. Over time, it becomes covered in soil and other **organic** matter. Carbon-14 is an element found in all living **organisms**. When organisms die, they stop making new carbon. Scientists compare the amount of carbon-14 in the organic matter of the soil sample to a living organism to find the age of the sample.

This image was taken by a GOES-17 satellite. GOES-17 is a series of weather satellites that detects and **monitors** storms, wildfires, and other natural events.

They can date samples up to 60,000 years old. Scientists also compare the dates of many samples to create a record of hurricanes that happened in the area in the past. They look for patterns that can help them tell when and where hurricanes might strike again.

Remote–Sensing Satellites

Scientists focus on finding out when the next hurricane will strike, as well as where it will strike and how strong it will be. Different countries around the world have a number of satellites placed at specific spots in the sky. The satellites provide nonstop images of the planet that scientists can use to track the location of storm systems. The satellites also use **radar** and **infrared sensors** to gather data, or information, about cloud patterns, temperature, rain, and wind speed.

Computer Models

Meteorologists use the data they gather to develop computer models. These allow them to figure out how strong the hurricane is and predict its path. They can forecast storm activity and alert people well before a hurricane strikes land. This technology helps reduce the risk to people, property, and animals.

This NASA satellite image shows Cyclone Vayu on June 11, 2019.

VICTIMS OF GLOBAL WARMING

Scientists are researching the impact **global warming** has on how often hurricanes take place and how powerful they are. In March 2019, Cyclone Idai made landfall in Mozambique. Then in June, Cyclone Vayu ripped through India, and in October, Typhoon Hagibis hit Japan.

As Earth's **atmosphere** gets warmer, the ocean's surface could become warmer too. Warm water is the fuel that makes hurricanes develop and grow. This could help explain why there were twice as many Category 4 and 5 hurricanes in the early 2000s than in the 1970s. Wind speeds and the time that hurricanes last has also increased in the past five decades.

Protecting People

Severe weather events can move quickly, so often there is not a lot of time to prepare. High-risk communities put special systems in place to help prevent disasters. Some systems give people time to protect their homes and move to safety. Others help stop hurricane damage from happening at all.

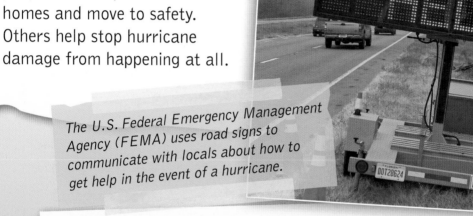

The U.S. Federal Emergency Management Agency (FEMA) uses road signs to communicate with locals about how to get help in the event of a hurricane.

Severe Weather Warning

In the United States, a system of alerts is used in hurricane-affected areas. Alerts are communicated using outdoor warning sirens, cell phone apps, local and cable TV channels, and radio stations. Devices—such as a National Oceanic and Atmospheric Administration (NOAA) weather radio—sound an alarm in the event of a storm warning. They usually run on batteries, so they work if there is no power.

Natural Solution

Many coastal areas are highly developed. In communities where there is a risk of storm surge, wetlands are often put in place to help reduce flood damage. Wetland plants help prevent **erosion** by binding soil to the ground and slowing the rush of waves and floodwaters. In 2012, wetlands prevented more than $625 million in potential damage when Hurricane Sandy struck the U.S. east coast.

Putting up Reinforcements

In some areas, communities require new buildings to be constructed using materials and designs that can withstand hurricane-force winds. In Miami, Florida, new buildings must be able to stand up to 130-mile-per-hour (209 kph) winds in high-risk areas. Other communities, such as New Orleans, have installed levees and floodwalls to protect against flooding. During Hurricane Katrina, more than 50 poorly designed and maintained levees and floodwalls failed. Today, the city has a system of drainage pumps and levees designed to prevent similar disasters.

Bubble Curtain

Scientists are working on a project that they hope will one day reduce the effect of hurricanes on land. This project involves the use of a "bubble curtain." It may be possible to place a pipe deep in the ocean and pump air through it to create a curtain of air bubbles. The bubbles would bring cold water from the depths of the ocean to mix with warm water at the surface. Cool water means less fuel for the hurricane. This technology, if possible, is still a long way from reality.

PROTECTING POTENTIAL VICTIMS

Hurricane hunters are people who fly into hurricanes to collect weather data and report on the condition of the storm. They collect data about wind speeds, rainfall, and air pressure within the storm and send it to the National Hurricane Center in Miami, Florida. They risk their lives to save thousands of others. In 2007, an unmanned aircraft system (UAV), called the Aerosonde, was sent into the eye of a hurricane for the first time. It sent **real-time** data to hurricane researchers.

In New Orleans, 192 miles (309 km) of levees and 99 miles (159 km) of floodwalls help hold back overflow from the Mississippi River.

ANTONIO'S STORY:
Rebuilding Our Lives

When we arrived in Naguabo, it was not good news. As we drove down what had been our street, I remember thinking I was going to be sick. There were piles of rubble where the houses once were. I kept hoping that maybe our house would be okay. I imagined the hurricane suddenly changing its path or coming to a stop just before it hit our house. But we weren't so lucky. Maria had destroyed our home, and my father's fishing boat was washed out to sea. But we were some of the lucky ones because we had each other. Many of our friends and family had been killed in the flooding.

The first weeks after Maria were the hardest. We sorted through the rubble looking for anything worth keeping. There wasn't much. What hadn't been destroyed was soaked with water. It was fall, and the nights were chilly. We had nothing but a blue **tarp** for shelter. Food was hard to come by. Clean water was even harder to find.

It took months after Hurricane Maria to restore power to everyone in Puerto Rico. The blackout was the largest in U.S. history and the second-largest in the world.

My father had no work since his boat was gone. Jobs were difficult to find, so it was hard to make money. We needed help to get by, and were lucky to get some money from FEMA. It wasn't much, but it was a start. My father began to rebuild our home. Our school was damaged during the hurricane, so we had no place to be during the day. It was boring sitting around with nothing to do. We had no power, so we couldn't even watch TV. It was months before the power was restored. Even now, it cuts out from time to time. We were very excited when our school reopened and we could get back to normal.

It has been a few years since Maria struck. I still get scared when it rains hard or the winds are strong. But I know things are getting better. Our little town banded together to help each other, and we get stronger every day.

After Maria, FEMA gave out almost 170,000 tarps as temporary shelters.

DANGER

Glossary

atmosphere The layer of gases that surrounds a planet

basins Dips in the land where rivers and their branches drain

carbon-14 dating A scientific method used to find the age of an object

climate change The long-term change in Earth's weather patterns

communities Groups of people who live in one place, such as a village or town

debris Waste or pieces of material left over from an event such as a disaster

deposited Placed or left something somewhere

ecosystem A system or community of plants and animals that live together

erosion The wearing away of something

evacuate To clear an area of people because it is dangerous

fictional Made up, not true

freshwater Water that is not salty

global warming The gradual increase in Earth's average temperature

infrared sensors Electronic devices that measure the infrared light coming from objects in their view

latitude The position of a place north or south of the equator

levees Barriers that prevent rivers from overflowing

monitors Observes or checks on the progress of something over a period of time

natural disaster A disaster caused by nature, not human-made

organic Natural, not human-made

organisms Living things

potential Something that might be possible in the future

pressure The force acting on a surface

radar A system used to detect radio waves to determine the angle, speed, and range of an object

real-time Something happening in the present moment

reinforced Something made stronger

satellites Human-made objects that send information from space to Earth

storm surge The rise in the sea level due to a storm

tarp A large sheet of waterproof material that is used as a cover

tropical Related to regions just north or south of the equator that are known for their warm, humid climates

tropical storms Storms that originate in the tropics and bring harsh winds and heavy rains

Learning More

Learn more about hurricanes and their dangers.

Books

Callender, Kacen, and Kheryn Callender. *Hurricane Child*. Scholastic, 2019.

Seigel, Rachel. *Hurricane Readiness*. Crabtree Publishing, 2019.

Shotz, Jennifer Li. *Hero: Hurricane Rescue*. HarperCollins, 2017.

Sillett, Julia. *Hurricanes Harvey, Irma, Maria, and Nate*. Crabtree Publishing, 2019.

Websites

Discover the science of how hurricanes happen at:
https://www.ducksters.com/science/earth_science/hurricanes.php

Find out what causes hurricanes at:
https://kids.nationalgeographic.com/explore/science/hurricane/

Learn more about how hurricanes work at:
https://science.howstuffworks.com/nature/natural-disasters/hurricane.htm

Discover more about how hurricanes form at:
www.weatherwizkids.com/weather-hurricane.htm

Index

About the Author

Heather C. Hudak has written hundreds of books for
children on all kinds of topics. When she is not writing,
Heather loves camping in the mountains near her home and
traveling around the world. In 2017, she was sailing in the
Caribbean when Hurricane Maria struck Puerto Rico.